Rational Reform
Adoption

Josh Bryant

Josh Bryant

For My Children
and all Children

Preface

In a hotel room one late September day in Kansas City, Missouri, my wife and I took a call we had been waiting for. We were at a missionary training conference hoping one day soon to live overseas for several years. We had a heart for people from all over the world. Motivated by our Christian faith and heart for the nations, we decided we would adopt a child transracially. We were waiting for a call from our adoption attorney to tell us there was an expectant mother who wanted to meet us.

On that call, we learned that a young lady was expecting in Northwest Arkansas where we lived. She was about four months along and was having a baby girl. The cost would be $25,000 (or so we were told). We had saved up and were ready to expand our family, so we agreed. We signed an engagement agreement and were on our way to adopt a baby girl.

Almost four years later, I was at a funeral when my wife called me. I ignored the call since I was otherwise indisposed. She immediately called back. We have this agreement that if we don't answer a call, we're in a meeting or otherwise can't talk. If one of us immediately calls back, we promise it is important enough to step out of a meeting. So as politely as I could, I excused myself from the funeral and took her call.

"There's a baby boy due in four days that doesn't have a home," my wife said.

I knew what that meant. We had been working for the past year to become foster parents. Everything was practically done; we would be an open foster home in a matter of days. Since we just had a home study, it should be relatively simple to use it for a private adoption. We agreed to pray about it for the day and make a decision in the morning.

When we woke up, we discussed it a bit more before work and agreed that this is where God was leading. I called and made the arrangements to meet the mother the next night for dinner. In the meantime, our family used every spare second to get ready. And what about our other two kids? An adoption this quick would be a shock to their system. We spent more time talking to them about the prospect of another child moving in. After a long day, we went to bed.

We slept well too. Usually, I hear the phone if it rings at night, even if it is just on vibrate. When we woke up the next morning, I had a dozen missed calls and several voicemails. The mother we were supposed to meet for dinner in nine hours had gone into labor at around 1:00 a.m. After I returned the first phone call, I couldn't believe it. The baby boy was born, and we were on our way to the hospital to adopt a baby that we'd only found out about 36-hours earlier.

Something wasn't quite right. The mom was very quiet. People she didn't seem to know came and went. The hospital social worker was abrasive. It just didn't quite add up. The next day we asked to speak with the social worker. She pulled us into an empty hospital room.

"What?" she asked.

I was a bit taken aback by her hostility even after seeing her attitude the day before.

"Look," I said. "If she doesn't want to do this, we don't want to either. She's very quiet, so we need your help to determine whether this is what she really wants to do."

Her posture immediately changed. She no longer had a scowl on her face, and the caustic attitude we'd seen for the last day was gone.

"Thank you for saying that," she said. "We never really know what to expect with adoptive parents through this agency."

I didn't exactly know what she meant. I didn't know any of the other adoptive parents, but I had heard rumors about the people we were dealing with. We didn't think any of that could be right though and certainly did not see any evidence of it ourselves.

"The truth is, she isn't sure about going through with an adoption," the social worker said. "She's still processing this, and because we have no history with her, it's hard to tell who is making decisions: her or someone else."

Again, I wasn't exactly sure what she was saying, but I knew that I didn't need to understand. I had come to trust social workers who had a chip on their shoulder as this woman had. As long as she was doing her job, everything would be fine. We left the room with the understanding that we would give the mother as much space as she needed and trust the social worker to tell us if there were problems.

We still got to spend time with the mother and develop a relationship with her. We prayed with her, asked her about her life and family, and answered any questions she had about us. In the end, she told us that she wasn't sure about adoption until she got to know us. Now that she knew us, she wanted us to adopt this baby boy. So, we did.

Not long went by before we heard more stories about adoption practitioners in the area. Each time we listened to an account, it got worse. Mothers who did not speak English did not understand that they may never see their child again. Mothers were intentionally working two adoption plans at the same time to get twice the pregnancy support. Unlicensed adoption practitioners were soliciting women for their children, offering $10,000 if they would agree to place their child for adoption. The smoke kept getting thicker and thicker; I knew that there had to be a fire somewhere.

Some colleagues of mine and I met to discuss the issues. There seemed to be conflicts of interest developing for adoption professionals in the area. We had heard stories about biological and adoptive parents from out of state meeting in Arkansas to perfect an adoption. Mothers were complaining of being harassed and threatened if they decided to parent their child. Something had to be done.

I went home and immediately started drafting adoption reform legislation. Once complete, I passed it around with my colleagues. We met with a local state legislator who was concerned about the problem and presented our ideas. He liked them and wanted some time to research them. We were on our way to seeing adoption reform.

Things never stay perfect forever. The legislator who was to be our champion was defeated in the general election by thirty votes. We quickly scrambled to present the legislation to other legislators with the blessing of our friend, who had been defeated but continued to work with us to see reform. Then was the task of convincing them it was as big of a problem as we thought it was. They agreed to run with the legislation, but that took time because it had to get officially transferred from one legislator to another. Then there were revisions to make. Finally, we had a bill on the floor of the Arkansas House of Representatives. We were making TV appearances and speaking up about the need for adoption reform. Things seemed to be going well.

A few days later, our son's biological mother sent me a message thanking me for speaking up about the issue of adoption reform. My heart sank. Why would she say that? Has she been a victim of this mess? Had we been sold a bill of goods? I couldn't just say, "you're welcome." I had to ask if everything we were told about her situation was accurate.

"You were told that?" she asked. "That's crazy."

It was as bad as I thought. She was unduly influenced to move to Arkansas on the promise of help when she got here. After she got here, that help was contingent upon her placing her child up for adoption and was manifest solely as a lump sum payment of $5,000. My heart sank further. She assured me that she had made the right decision, that she was glad we adopted her baby and were taking such good care of him. It did little to lift my spirits.

After our conversation ended, I began to cry. Then I got angry. Then I was more motivated than ever before. This had to stop.

Through it all, we fell one vote short in the Senate Judiciary Committee from getting our legislation through. This was a first for me (and everyone else who was not a legislator). We made some rookie mistakes that lead to more opposition than was necessary. We were able to get a compromise bill through on the last day of the session that made particular conduct criminal, but the system in which that conduct was carried out was as broken as ever.

We need to have a national conversation about adoption. We had no adoption laws until 1851. At that time, children were either informally adopted with no governmental influence, or they were adopted formally through a decree of the state legislature or by deed. You read that correctly – children were adopted by signing a deed in the same way property is transferred by signing a deed. Adoption was chiefly motivated by the need for cheap labor on the western frontier or a male heir to carry on the family line.

You would think things have gotten better by now, and in reality, they have. However, we still live in a nation in which it costs twice as much to adopt a Caucasian baby than it does to adopt an African American baby. Researchers have asked why there is such a cost disparity based on race. They discovered adoption professionals who unabashedly acknowledged that there are more African American babies available for adoption and fewer people who are willing to adopt them. There's an economic term for that: supply and demand.

Then you look at the issues that lead us to push adoption reform in Arkansas. People were being coerced or harassed into placing their child up for adoption. This was human trafficking. Some objected to that moniker at first. Then came just a few weeks before I started writing this book. One of the adoption practitioners we had heard the most about was arrested on more than sixty criminal counts in three jurisdictions, all related to fraudulent adoption practices.

The media went nuts. They found as many as twelve pregnant women in a three-bedroom house with only three mattresses in the entire house, leaving nine women to sleep on the floor. When TV cameras got inside the house, images of bedroom doors with padlocks on the outside flashed across my screen. Prosecutors held press conferences and stated that there were other investigations ongoing and that more indictments were likely. Finally, the cabal was coming down.

We were having national discussions, alright. I spoke with reporters from Arkansas, Arizona, Utah, Colorado, and Hawaii. My colleagues spoke with others, and I talked to the Attorneys General in several states. I suppose that would not have happened had I not jumped into action with my colleagues. We realized there were potentially dozens of women and adoptive families frightened out of their minds; the only person they had talked to had been arrested. I filed a lawsuit against the arrested man to consolidate all of his then-pending adoption cases in one court; one judge would ensure that each of them started from scratch and proceeded ethically.

Fights have persisted legislatively and through litigation. Progress is in the making, but we have a long way to go. Adoption in America is broken. In Arkansas, we hope to have it fixed by the middle of 2021. However, this is not just a problem in Arkansas. This is a national problem. There are conflicts of interest everywhere. There are unlicensed adoption practitioners whose only knowledge of the adoption process is their own journey helping others adopt. They have no idea how much pain the biological family is experiencing and providing no services at all to support them. In many states, unlawful payments are being facilitated under the table. Things have gotten so bad that national leaders in adoption circles have called for national standards of practice. National magazines have reported that some mothers now find an abortion less morally reprehensible than an adoption. If adoption is to continue as a means of child welfare, we need to have a serious conversation.

This book aims to start that conversation. It is not an exhaustive work by any stretch of the imagination. It is the first of what I imagine will be many editions. My goal is to bring to light the most egregious problems that I have encountered in the process of seeking adoption reform. Knowing the problem, I also aim to provide solutions to that problem. I will not claim to be the be-all and end-all in systematic adoption and ethics. However, I have devoted a great deal of time and energy to this project. Even still, I hope others have even better ideas. I hope together we can come up with ideas that will make adoption child-centric. I hope we can find solutions that at least end the ill effects of conflicts of interest if not do away with those conflicts altogether. I hope we can find the best way to ensure that the children in utero are given the best shot at life without the adults engaging (knowingly or unknowingly) in conduct that looks like the buying and selling of children. I hope we can find a way to ensure every life is equally priceless and not driven by market forces. I hope we can find ways to criminalize and punish those who have no training or experience in the multi-disciplinary complexity of adoption. At these targets, this book aims.

I
Rethinking the Triad

Among adoption professionals, the phrase "adoption triad" is often used as a way to define the three parties involved in an adoption: the child, the biological family, and the adoptive family. It is at times metaphorically described as a three-legged stool; it collapses without all three components. Sometimes it is referred to only like a triangle with one party at each of the three points. All are equal; all participate.

We in America need to rethink that triad; none of these metaphors describe what is or what should be in adoption. At times in our history, one leg of the stool was so insignificant that it might as well have never existed. One part of the triangle was so marginalized that its angle was far more acute than that of the adoptive and biological families. I refer to children "adopted" by a quitclaim deed so that the beneficiary of that deed would have labor out on the western frontier or a male heir by which the family name could go on. Even today, this leg of the stool does not touch the floor, and its angle is narrower than those of the adoptive parents and biological family.

As seen by the tragedy described in the preface, there are times in which the biological families are marginalized. That leg of the stool is not equal with the other two legs; that angle of the triangle is not the same size as the other angles. Far too often, the only leg that is too big – the only angle that is too wide – is that belonging to the adoptive family. Never has there been a time in American history in which the adoption system worked to ensure those three legs on the stool are equal in length and importance. There has never been a time in which the regime made sure that angles of the triangle were equal. The only thing that makes adoption work in these conditions are those adoption professionals who know what they are doing. They know when to saw a leg down a bit and broaden the angle of one.

Should it even be the case that the system works to ensure equality? I argue, no. Where in the Constitution is it written that adoptive parents should have the same rights to a child as the biological parents? Where is it written that the child in a mother's womb has no place in the discussion? Why should our adoption system generate a two-dimensional shape or a three-dimensional object on which people place their butts?

No – our adoption system should not be thought of in this way. Doing so does not describe the current state of affairs, nor does it represent the way things should be. Our system must be designed to create an adoption pyramid. An adoption pyramid does not describe adoption as it is now either.

Most of the time, the most important party is the adoptive parents. Their desire to adopt a child is praised while the biological family's desire to place a child up for adoption is given lip service at best and usually pitied. Their needs and wants are paramount. When an adoption fails, their emotional fall out is mourned, and the decision of the biological family is condemned. Sometimes we overcompensate and try to make the biological family the most important part of the pyramid. That's an awful lot of pressure on a couple making a tough decision under challenging circumstances. It can create situations in which a mother is applauded for deciding to parent when the motive all along has been to milk money out of an adoptive parent without getting caught. Either way you look at it, it is a goofy looking pyramid right now, and in none of these cases has an unborn child even been considered.

However, a pyramid does describe adoption as it should be. As a society, we must think of adoption in such a fashion that the child is considered as the most crucial party. That leg of the stool should be the longest; that angle of the triangle should be the widest. For open adoption to work, it is essential that adoptive and birth parents stay focused on the best interests of the adoptee. Adoption is about the child; decisions must be made consistent with the child's best interests.

Adoptive parents are not the most critical piece of the pyramid; they are not even the second most important piece of the pyramid. The most important party to an adoption is a defenseless, helpless, precious, innocent child who should form the foundation of our adoption pyramid. Every decision must be about that child. Before we are even thinking about an adoption, we must be thinking about prenatal care. When it's finally appropriate to start thinking about an adoption, we must consider what is in the child's best interests. Is an open adoption or a closed adoption best for the child? Is a five-day waiting period or a thirty-day waiting period best for the child? Is paying the biological family's rent in the best interest of the child, or should we be ok with the biological family living on the streets? Is buying healthy food in the best interest of the child, or should we require the biological mother to subsist on rice and beans only? In the vast majority of adoptions, the conversation centers around the money an adoptive family can pay and the money a biological family can get. This is because the system does not allow payment of expenses or does not restrict the amount of expenses in any meaningful way. The needs of the child are an afterthought at best.

The second most important party in the pyramid is the biological family. Our Supreme Court has decided that it is a fundamental, Constitutional right to have and raise children. As such, that right cannot be taken away without a compelling government interest by actions that are not narrowly tailored to meet that interest. If we make the importance of the biological parents too broad, we strip the government of the ability to protect abused and neglected children. If we make it too narrow, we give the government the ability to place a child up for adoption arbitrarily. For the pyramid to look right, and for adoption to work correctly, there must be just the right proportion of the importance of the biological family to the importance of the child.

The least important party in the pyramid are the adoptive parents. If we make them more critical than they should be, we give them the ability to override the will of the biological family. If we don't make them important enough, we minimize the financial and emotional investment and sacrifices made by adoptive parents to add to their family. As with biological parents to children, there must be just the right proportion of the importance of the adoptive parents to the importance of the biological family. Only then can we have a pyramid that looks right.

There are ways we can employ a legal system capable of ensuring the right balance. First, we must create systems that block economic forces from the process of adoption. Adoption is currently a marketplace, not a means of child welfare. It is about an adoptive family growing their family or having a child after struggling with infertility. When that is the case, a demand-driven marketplace is created. Taking care of a child is secondary to adopting a child within the racial, gender, and circumstantial parameters set by the adoptive parents. When that happens, economic forces take over because it is more challenging to match a child to some adoptive families with very restrictive parameters than to a family with few or no parameters. Things get even more complicated when more adoptive parents desire babies with specific characteristics than are available. We'll discuss this more in Chapter 2.

Secondly, we must design a system that provides for accountability the moment adoptive parents and biological parents make a connection. Most often in the United States, that connection is made in the offices of a third party – an agency or attorney. In a perfect system of child welfare that can work, but it doesn't work because there is no such ideal system. In the marketplace that we have, the agency or attorney does not look like a social services provider or a child welfare advocate: it looks like a brokerage. Biological parents go to an agency to place a child; adoptive parents go there to adopt one. Likewise, home buyers go to a real estate broker who happens to have sellers lined up ready to sell their homes. This type of dual representation divides loyalties at best; at worst, it places the middleman's interests above everyone else's. The pyramid doesn't even resemble a triangle anymore; it's now an adoption quadrangle. Everyone must have their voice; sometimes, even the child. Attorneys or agencies with the singular loyalty of their clients can hold each other accountable to stave off the abuses that we've seen. We'll discuss this more in Chapter 3.

Thirdly, we must back away from the notion that all monies paid from adoptive parents to biological parents are consideration in the purchase of a child. Several states prohibit the payment of any funds from adoptive families to biological families. The United States is even party to a treaty that prohibits such payments, although the federalist nature of our government prevents the federal government from doing much about it. If we are genuinely concerned primarily about the best interests of the child, we must allow adoptive parents to ensure that the child is safe financially. Without that financial support, children are likely to start life behind the eight ball. My colleagues and I have seen the children who do not receive prenatal care because the agency or attorney was working with did not take them to the doctor and pocketed the money that the adoptive parents paid for prenatal care. They are sickly with immune systems that do not respond fast enough to the common cold. They have weight gain problems or neurological difficulties. Our adoption systems can work to ensure that is not the case. We'll discuss how more in Chapter 4.

We must have a set of national standards to which adoption practitioners are trained, licensed, monitored, and disciplined. That system at present is weak. Those who have no training or do not otherwise meet state standards to run an adoption agency become adoption consultants. They often take the place of an agency on the promise of saving an adoptive family money. They'll usually work with an attorney who will be the official person lawfully placing, planning to place, or assisting in placing a child for adoption. However, with no training in social work, mental health, or law, they often distort the pyramid. They market to adoptive families in a way that perpetuates the falsehood that the adoptive parents are the most essential part of the pyramid. They can cause a lot of damage. What's worse is that while in many states these practices are illegal, there are fragile enforcement mechanisms in place. We'll talk about this more in Chapter 5.

We must get away from the notion that adoptive parents should have the final say in all matters after the adoption is finalized. Indeed, there is a bundle of parental rights that should be absolute: discipline, religious upbringing, education, medical care, and so forth. However, the research is clear that when we take that authority to the extreme of forbidding contact between the child and biological parents, we harm everyone involved. The research is clear that as children grow older and ask questions about their heritage, those who have been raised in closed adoptions struggle with identity formation. Research shows that biological families (and mothers in particular) struggle more with post-partum depression, guilt, and other mental health issues in closed adoptions than in open ones. In what may surprise many adoptive families, research shows that in the end, open adoption is healthier for them as well. Their relationship with their child is not nearly as strained as it often is when, in teenage years, they prohibit the child from knowing their biological parents. We'll discuss this in Chapter 6.

Along those lines, we must also not back away from the concept of the home study. In talking with many policymakers and adoptive parents, I sometimes hear the argument that home studies should be eliminated because the only thing required for anyone else to have a child is to have sex. That is an argument that makes the adoptive parents more critical than they should be in this process. Properly completed home studies can be very effective in helping biological families feel comfortable with their decision to place their child up for adoption. They help the courts protect children by ending adoption plans involving a felon or convicted sex offender. They help prepare adoptive families for the burdens of parenthood by forcing them to talk about the state of their marriage, the likelihood of conflict and divorce, budgets and financial considerations, and others in the family. We must maintain the home study as part of our adoption system.

This is not an exhaustive list of what can be done, but whatever solutions we have to fix our broken adoption system must have the best interests of the child as the goal. Those interests should be followed by the rights and needs of the biological parents, and finally, the desires and dreams of the adoptive parents. Any other paradigm by which we construct a system of adoption is lopsided and carries with it the risk of grave injustices.

II
Supply and Demand

One of the most prominent stains that remains on the institution of adoption is the cost. I do not argue that those professionals who assist others in an adoption should not be paid for their services, far from it. I do argue that those professionals should not be paid for a product.

Studies have shown that the cost of private adoptions to adopt a Caucasian child is approximately $40,000. Most studies show that the cost to adopt an African American child is half of that or less. Researchers have asked why there is such a cost disparity by race, and adoption professionals in many cases have unabashedly answered. There are more African American babies available for adoption and fewer adults who are willing to adopt them. In other words, supply is higher than demand, so the cost is lower. For Caucasian babies, demand is higher than supply; thus, the price is higher. These same forces determine the value of food, clothes, real estate, and almost everything else we consume as a society.

As we have already discussed, adoption is not a means of child welfare. As it stands, adoption is a marketplace. There are scholarly economic analyses of the cost of adoption that go so far as to determine which parameters of the adoptive parents cause the most considerable degree of increase in price. Agencies and attorneys spend millions of dollars a year on advertising. There are national, for-profit agencies that have branches. Some reportedly follow a franchise model. It is big business that primarily targets the demand with the industry message and sometimes goes to extremes to obtain a supply.

Let's get the worst-case scenario out of the way first. Wholesalers and retailers are always looking for the best price on their supply. We've seen the harm that can do in consumer products. Sometimes the corners that are cut to obtain the best price decrease the quality such that consumers are harmed by the product. Sometimes those corners mean that the product is made by a 12-year-old overseas working 14-hours six days every week for less than a dollar per day. Sometimes those corners mean that factory conditions are unsafe, and workers are harmed in industrial accidents.

What happens when adoption operates this way? For years in Northwest Arkansas, there has been a large contingent of people from the Republic of the Marshall Islands. Under a treaty called the Compact of Free Association, Marshallese people can come and go in the United States and even work here without a visa. They moved to Northwest Arkansas to work in chicken plants; their population and influence have continued to grow. Since they can come and go freely, some adoption practitioners saw an opportunity.

One such practitioner has been accused (as of the writing of this book) of offering pregnant women $10,000 to place their child for adoption, flying them to the United States for that sole purpose, and housing them in deplorable conditions. They were sometimes crammed 12-deep into a three-bedroom house with only three beds in the house. That left nine women to sleep on the floor. They reported to authorities that they were treated like property. The United States Attorney for the Western District of Arkansas Mr. Duane "Dak" Kees unequivocally called this human trafficking in its purest form.

In other states, this individual is accused of charging adoptive parents for the medical expenses of the biological parents while fraudulently filing Medicaid applications on behalf of the biological mothers. The money he charged the adoptive parents for medical expenses increased his margins by over $800,000 according to estimates of the State of Arizona. By some estimates, this accounts for more than 200 adoptions.

Other practitioners do the same things, lawyers and unlicensed individuals alike. When a mother has second thoughts and expresses a desire to parent, the muscle is sent in to clarify things. The mother is threatened with jail time, deportation, and more. Many times, mothers do not get what they are promised because a facilitator skims money off the top. We've even encountered mothers who were forced to have sex with a facilitator in exchange for their support payment.

After birth, the mother is often cut loose. She has no command of the English language to speak of and no appreciable job skills. She probably does not have a driver's license, which would not do her any good anyway because she does not have a car. Sleeping on couches in already cramped quarters with no way to make money, mothers often resort to the only way they've seen available in America. They get pregnant and enter into an adoption plan. Twelve is the most children I have seen a mother place for adoption. She was under the age of thirty-five at that time and almost died giving birth.

This environment was created by adoption practitioners who act as the paragons of retail adoption. They have single-handedly increased supply. As a result, demand has even gone up. None of these adoption practitioners are scrounging around for clients. They have the supply and the demand flocks to them. Some of them claim the ability to do things at a cheaper rate, and at one point, that was undoubtedly true. Now, however, they do not chiefly attract business from the saving of money. Their value proposition is the saving of time. You can adopt a Marshallese baby in six months. Many going through more traditional routes sometimes wait six years.

This is not just a Marshallese problem. In fighting for adoption reform, we have encountered victims from every marginalized population in America: Caucasians, Latinos, African Americans – no race, ethnicity, or nationality has a monopoly on victimhood in fraudulent adoptions. For every market, there is a black market. In the adoption market, babies are trafficked. Mothers are smuggled. We've even heard reports from government agencies that they have encountered teenage girls who were pressured into getting pregnant so they can put their child up for adoption. Fraud is rampant, and few report it in fear of getting caught themselves. Corners are cut. Supply chains are stretched to the max. People get hurt — some die.

The problems outlined in this book are interconnected. We have already discussed the role of pregnancy-related expense payments in the effort to increase margins among some adoption practitioners. We will review it more in Chapter 4. When we worked to see each party in an adoption have their own attorney, the chief objection we encountered was that it would increase the cost. In other words, practitioners were unwilling to see a decrease in margins; their margins were more critical than being held accountable for ethical adoption practices. They spoke on behalf of all adoptive parents in objecting to an increase in costs that they would pass along to adoptive parents. However, most adoptive parents we talked to were fine with the cost increases if it meant that the adoption system would have checks and balances. We'll discuss this issue more in the next chapter.

When margin becomes a problem, the easiest people to marginalize are the biological parents. Unethical adoption practitioners save money by not providing appropriate services to the biological parents. The best agencies working with biological families offer job training, counseling, and other social services. When market forces (including sheer greed) dictate that margins increase, good business sense says that advertising is the last thing you cut. Greed says your profit is also far from the chopping block. Instead, one or two counseling sessions are cut here and there. A doctor's appointment or two are canceled or conveniently missed. A couple of hundred dollars are skimmed off of the support payments. Books are cooked. Nobody will know, especially since there is no one solely loyal to the biological family to ensure that those paid by the adoptive family are meeting their obligations.

Several possible solutions have been proposed. To understand them, we need to know how a service is priced. There are three models. The first is cost-based pricing. In this model, the cost of the service is calculated per project or period of time. The question answered is, "how much does it cost to operate for one hour?" or "how much does it cost to complete one adoption?" Advanced analyses account for seasonal fluctuations and more complicated cases. Once the agency has a number, a margin is added to arrive at the cost of the service on an hourly or per-project basis.

The second is market- or competition-based pricing. In this model, the sole factor is the price at which the agency's competitors are offering the same service. It is strictly based on competing for clients and works in two directions. On the one hand, it can work to push prices down when the number of professionals offering the service is also high. On the other hand, when too few offer the service, it has the opposite effect. Professionals could perform the service for $20,000, but because they see their competitors providing that service for $40,000, they decide they can offer it for $35,000 and increase their margins while still beating out the competition. The latter is usually the case in the adoption industry.

The final model is the value-based pricing model. In this model, professionals only consider the perceived value of the service to the client. This is complicated because it considers the value of the service in isolation and not usually in relation to other options available to the client. It is especially tricky in the adoption industry because, for some clients, the alternatives are pregnancy often covered by an insurance product. Under the primary model today, where the adoption agency's message is typically targeted towards the adoptive parents, reaching couples who can conceive requires pricing that is equal to the cost after insurance plus the value of adopting over giving birth including the intrinsic value of adopting and the benefits of avoiding the pains and stresses of pregnancy.

Missing from this analysis so far is the adoption pyramid. What do current pricing models say about our focus in the adoption industry? Each of the three pricing models eliminates the biological mother and the baby from the equation. The cost-based approach emphasizes the practitioner's margins. Since the highest cost is typically focused on the health of the biological mother and baby, clearly, this model tends to eliminate them from the foundation of the pyramid. This either focuses on the adoptive parents and makes them the essential component of the pyramid, or it focuses on the practitioner. The market-based approach doesn't consider anyone but the practitioner. It's all about getting the best price and being the most competitive among other adoption practitioners. The value-based approach is strictly focused on the adoptive parents. How much are they willing to pay, and how much am I willing to do for that price?

Applying these pricing models to the pyramid shows that none of the pricing models is in and of itself is helpful in the adoption system. It is too easy to manipulate the cost of adoption by eliminating support for the biological parents, which either decreases the cost of the adoption or increases the margin of the adoption practitioner. As we have already seen, the market-based approach is a double-edged sword with the potential to lower the cost of adoption or increase it. Additionally, the market-based approach is, to some degree, responsible for racial cost disparities. Finally, the value-based model fails to consider different client segments (fertile, infertile, values motivated, etc.) to set a fair price adequately. A completely new service industry pricing model is necessary.

With appropriate regulation, the cost-based model could work well and still leave room for free-market competition under the market-based model. The law can require the provision of certain services to biological parents to establish a common baseline for adoption practitioners. For example, the law can require a certain number of counseling sessions, the provision of basic nutritional requirements for a healthy pregnancy, the provision of prenatal care, and programs geared toward career development, family planning, and other social services. Each service required by law would need to meet specific quality standards as well to prevent adoption practitioners from seeking out the cheapest and least qualified services. Such a construct sets a minimum cost of service among all adoption practitioners that cares chiefly for the health and well-being of the child, followed closely by the requisite health and well-being of the biological mother. On that baseline adoption practitioners can build additional programs that add value and cost to the adoption in a competitive format under the market-based pricing model.

While fighting for adoption reform, we attempted to implement at least some of these measures. The chief complaint we got was that the approach was too paternalistic. What if the biological family does not want counseling? Must the government force it on them? Of course not. Everything in this process of adoption must be voluntary. The law can still require adoption practitioners to provide counseling and biological families to waive their right to receive that service in writing. As long as practitioners are not actively dissuading adoptive families from obtaining the counseling, those families who voluntarily decline counseling increase the practitioner's margins or decrease the cost to adoptive parents. The latter certainly appears to be the more ethical course.

This would not necessarily end all racial price disparities. Agencies would still have the flexibility to charge less for services offered in the adoption of an African American child based on the lesser effort required to make a match. However, that disparity is far more palatable to most because the cost is based on the time and effort expended by the agency, not based on the supply and demand for a child of a specific race. The disparity would also be far narrower than it is because the same services offered to Caucasian biological parents would be provided to African American biological parents. The cost to the adoption practitioner would remain the same.

As an additional check on adoption practitioners, biological families should have their own attorneys or adoption advocates working to ensure that they receive the best services possible within reason. This has the added benefit of ending conflicts of interest that currently exist within the adoption industry and all of the social ills that accompany them. It also aids in the process of ensuring proper adoption-related expenses are paid and aids in the process of establishing the terms of an open adoption. These will be discussed in Chapters 4 and 6, respectively.

Regulators would also need additional authority and must evaluate adoption practitioners on a new level. The services biological families are provided must be adequate. Records must be kept. Practitioners must be held to a standard of accountability in the services they provide to biological families. This will be discussed further in Chapter 5.

Applying this model to the adoption pyramid is shows a much more balanced image. The focus is on the child. The required services are designed to give the child the best chance at a healthy start to life. The next priority is the biological family. They receive counseling and services necessary to help them deal with the emotional and psychological difficulties in adoption and the situation that lead them to the conclusion that adoption was the best course forward. Lastly, the next priority is the adoptive parents. They have assurances that the pricing is fair, the process is ethical, and the practitioner is subject to at least some checks and balances.

Researchers uncovered other rationales for racial price disparities as well that had less to do with supply and demand but were equally deplorable. Some practitioners described the difference between the cost to adopt a Caucasian baby and the cost to adopt an African

American baby as a subsidy. Those who could afford to adopt a Caucasian baby subsidized those who could not.

This is not an acceptable financial analysis either. It fails to remedy the perception or belief that infants of some races are worth less than those of other races. It adds the implication that infants of some races are second class goods. It is as if infants in some races are the private brand product, and infants in other races are the designer brand. Consumers buy the product they can afford. Even if this were an accurate description of the economic forces in play, the same solutions that balance the equation in a supply and demand context balance the equation in the context of a private subsidy.

While bearing little on the supply and demand issues in current adoption practice, it is worth briefly reviewing the impact tax policy has on adoptions. Until recently, adoptive families received a refundable tax credit of around $14,000. That means that the entirety of the $14,000 in addition to the tax refund was paid to the adoptive family. In 2017, Congress reduced that to a non-refundable tax credit. The credit can only zero out your annual tax liability. If an adoptive family paid in $8,000 and got a $4,000 refund without the tax credit, they would only get an $8,000 refund, not an $18,000 refund. This does not come into the analysis of the racial disparity because the tax credit is applied equally to adoptive parents. It has nothing to do with the race of the child.

It does raise an interesting prospect, however. Since we are already using tax policy to incentivize adoption, can we use tax policy to disincentivize disparities in price based on the race of the child? To this question, I must answer no. If done, there are several possibilities.

Congress could make the tax credit refundable if an adoptive couple adopts a minority child. The goal would be to increase demand for African American children. However, such a system would likely fail to survive constitutional scrutiny. Furthermore, as demand goes up, the price would go up as well with no guarantee that the larger tax refund would offset that cost. Even still, the underlying value disparity would still exist. It would be masked by what amounts to a government subsidy. This would continue to require us to use supply and demand economics to understand the pricing environment. It would fail by itself to place the child as the most important party on the adoption pyramid; instead, the adoptive parents' desire to be fiscally responsible drives the decision. This approach does not solve the problem.

Congress could begin to phase out the tax credit past a particular cost of adoption to reduce demand and lower the price for Caucasian babies. The intended result would be, in essence, to cap the cost of adoption based on people's aversion to giving the government money. However, people would still pay higher prices to get a child that met their desired characteristics and forfeit the tax refund in the process. It would have the benefit of seeing costs go down with demand, but it still requires a supply and demand approach to the pricing model. It also fails to account for extraordinary circumstances in which medical problems or other unusual issues increase the suitability of higher amounts of pregnancy support payments. It, too, fails to put the child at the focus of everyone's efforts; the adoptive parents would be even more predominant under this system. This model would be more likely to survive constitutional scrutiny as not patently race-based, and generally, there are fewer downsides to this approach than the prior one, but it still fails to accomplish the goal of reducing or eliminating racial cost disparities.

Other approaches have been discussed as well: taxing adoption practitioners on revenue per adoption above a certain threshold, fixing the price of adoptions, and different less likely scenarios. Taxing adoption practitioners requires more bureaucracy and invites tax fraud. Setting the price of adoptions likely raises the costs for many and tempts practitioners to do everything they can to decrease their costs – usually at the expense of biological families. Tax policy is not the solution.

Perhaps someone has a better idea than these as the means of ending racial price disparities in American adoptions while placing priority on the child, followed by the biological family, followed by the adoptive family. Until that idea comes forward, establishing a minimum standard of service that adoption practitioners must provide allows for a hybrid cost- and competition-based pricing system for a service, staves off supply and demand economic forces in adoption pricing, and more importantly works towards a healthy child, the health and dignity of the biological family, and protects adoptive families at the same time.

III
Conflicts of Interest

Most of the time, adoption practitioners market their services to both adoptive and biological parents. As a result, both adoptive and biological parents are assisted by the same practitioner. This practice inherently generates a conflict of interest. In a majority of situations, this arrangement works just fine based on the personal ethics of the practitioner. However, in some cases, it creates substantial problems for everyone involved in the pyramid.

Naturally, one would think that the practitioner's loyalties lie with the adoptive parents. They are the party of the pyramid paying the bills. However, think about the situation in which one biological family returns to the same practitioner for multiple adoptions to different adoptive parents. If the practitioner places four children up for adoption for the biological family, the practitioner is paid by four different sets of adoptive parents but serves one biological family four times. Relationships are formed between the biological family and the practitioner, and in the worst-case scenarios (whether consciously or subconsciously), the practitioner sees the biological family as little more than a supply chain. In other words, assuming the average $40,000 cost for an adoption, the biological family is single-handedly responsible for $160,000 in revenue to the practitioner when any given adoptive family is only responsible for $40,000 in revenue. Now it isn't so clear where the practitioner's loyalties lie.

Before we go much further, let us analyze this situation through the lens, which is our adoption pyramid. Where is the adopted child? Statistically, there will be practitioners who are more concerned with the child than they are with the adoptive or biological parents, regardless of how much money either brings to the practitioner. However, human nature and the need to earn a living will, in at least some cases, make the practitioner's loyalty shift away from the unborn child. Peruse a few adoption agency websites and see how many of them are geared towards the health and wellbeing of the child. The vast majority of the content on adoption agency websites is about the benefits of adoption to the adoptive or biological families: the services offered to the biological mother, the joy of expanding the adoptive family, and so forth. Even in situations where both adoptive and biological families have their own representation and advisors, few give as much thought to the child as they give everyone else. This makes the pyramid shaky at best; the foundation – the child – is not nearly as broad as the segments, which are the adoptive or biological families.

Notwithstanding the lack of focus on the child, when loyalties are divided, the pyramid loses its form. If the practitioner's loyalties lie primarily with the adoptive parents, the top of the pyramid is wider than the middle and bottom of the pyramid. When the practitioner's loyalties lie with the biological parents, the center of the pyramid is wider than the top than is appropriate. In each of these scenarios, the pyramid is not a pyramid at all. How can we restore the shape of the pyramid?

The most obvious solution is to ensure all parts of the pyramid have independent representation and advisors. Someone must fight to ensure that throughout the process of adoption, everyone keeps their eye on the foundation of the pyramid – the child. If the adoptive family fails to provide appropriate support to the biological family (specifically the mother) and the child stands to suffer without that support, someone needs to step in and fight for proper support.

Likewise, the biological family should have representation that seeks support as well. If the biological family is doing things that would harm the child like refusing prenatal care or using drugs, someone needs to step in and fight for the child. Likewise, the adoptive family who stands to suffer in caring for the child subject to such harmful things should have a say in the matter.

The chief objection to this course of action has been that it would raise the cost of adoption. This is a rather short-sighted objection in that it only considers the cost of the adoption itself. Those who hold to this objection fail to consider that the actual cost of an adoption could not be finally tabulated until the child is no longer a child; until the child is wholly self-sustaining and no longer reliant on the aid of the adoptive family. The latest estimates place the cost of raising a child at anywhere between $225,000 and $270,000, not including the price of a college education. Add the initial cost of adopting a child and the cost of college education, and the number rises to anywhere from $265,000 to $370,000 or more on average.

We cannot expect that in an adoption process in which the biological family does not have the support to obtain prenatal care or is using drugs during the pregnancy, these numbers would be average. How much do we add in medical costs to the adoptive family? One of our adopted children had suspect prenatal care if any at all. Getting hold of any record of prenatal care proved impossible in our case. At two months of age, our child stopped eating. He did not gain weight. We tried other (more expensive) formulas and thickening agents. We tried adding oil to the formula to give it a caloric boost. Nothing we tried worked. We spent our first week in the hospital at four months of age. There was no change. Less than a month later, we had a battery of tests done by almost a dozen pediatric specialists. No change. Two months later, we were back in the hospital for a two-week stay at which we had to begin feeding him through a nasogastric tube. A month later, we were at the Mayo clinic for surgeries and another battery of tests from another dozen doctors or so. No change. Two months later, we were back in the hospital for two weeks precipitated by profuse and constant vomiting. This time they scheduled surgery and placed a gastrostomy tube to deliver food. Seven months later (with an intervening trip to the children's hospital for follow up visits) over the Christmas and New Year's holidays, we spent almost three weeks in the hospital. Our child crashed. Oxygen saturation was in the 60s, and the breaths we saw were what the pulmonologists called "rescue breaths."

Intubation ensued, followed by days of chemical sedation in the PICU (pediatric intensive care unit). Since then, we've been in the hospital at least twice a year with pneumonia or other strange anomalies. We've been to the best doctors in the world at Boston Children's Hospital (tied to Harvard Medical School). They referred us to the Undiagnosed Disease Network, which after months of reviewing the case, determined that humanity was unlikely to develop the necessary technology or medical knowledge to provide a diagnosis any time soon. Thank God for insurance. Between weeks at a time away from work for hospital visits, and bills from hospital visits, the cost to raise this child will be in the millions of dollars. Given a choice, we'd have gladly spent more to start the adoption than we did had that expense ensured prenatal care and someone to fight for our child before birth.

Another objection to this course of action has been that it would make the adoption process adversarial. I have news for you: as long as the adoption process has involved a judge, it has been an adversarial process. See this phrase from the United States Constitution:

> The judicial Power shall extend to all Cases, in Law and Equity, arising under this Constitution, the Laws of the United States, and Treaties made, or which shall be made, under their Authority;—to all Cases affecting Ambassadors, other public ministers and Consuls;—to all Cases of admiralty and maritime

Jurisdiction;—to Controversies to which the United States shall be a Party;—to Controversies between two or more States;—between a State and Citizens of another State;—between Citizens of different States;—between Citizens of the same State claiming Lands under Grants of different States, and between a State, or the Citizens thereof, and foreign States, Citizens or Subjects.

Article III, Section 2, United States Constitution

Every state has similar language in their constitutions except in very narrow circumstances that do not apply to the issue of adoptions.

In short, any case before a judge must involve an actual injury, without which the plaintiffs or petitioners have no standing in the Court. In adoptions, what is the harm? One party has a child and the Constitutional right to raise that child; another party wants that right. There is your case or controversy. It is by its very nature adversarial, which brings up another point specific to lawyers.

The American Bar Association wrote the Model Rules of Professional Conduct. Most states have adopted at least portions (if not most or all) of the model rules. Rule 1.7 prohibits an attorney from engaging in a concurrent conflict of interests. A concurrent conflict of interests exists when: "(1) the representation of one client will be directly adverse to another client; or (2) there is a significant risk that the representation of one or more clients will be materially limited by the lawyer's responsibilities to another client, a former client or a third person or by a personal interest of the lawyer.

The first question is whether, under the circumstances described in this chapter, the attorney represents both the adoptive family and the biological family. While an attorney could get by only representing the adoptive family, it is neither wise nor likely. At some point, that attorney must have the biological family sign consents to the adoption. That consent will have serious legal implications, terminating their parental rights forever. The attorney cannot answer questions about the document or give them advice on whether to sign it or not. If an attorney does that, an attorney-client relationship has probably formed whether either intended such a relationship. Even if the attorney offers no such advice, no one wants to answer the ethics complaint of a biological family who claims the contrary.

Additionally, lawyers can only place a child up for adoption because they are a lawyer. If they were not a licensed attorney, they would have to meet the qualifications to be a licensed placement agency in their state, which usually requires a background in social work. Under those conditions, the act of placing, assisting in placing, or planning in placing the child of another up for adoption, the lawyer is providing a legal service. If there was a question as to whether an attorney-client relationship has been formed at the signing of consent, there is no reasonable argument that one has not begun the moment the attorney agrees to place a child up for adoption.

When the attorney then contracts with an adoptive family to represent them in the adoption of the child the attorney is placing for adoption on behalf of the biological family, the representation of that adoptive family is directly adverse to biological family and vice versa. Even if it is only indirectly adverse, the relationship generates a substantial risk that the representation of the other would materially limit the representation of one client. What if the biological parents decide to withdraw from the adoption plan? The attorney must then assist the biological parents in revoking that consent. Is the attorney's ability to do so limited by the relationship with the adoptive family? Of course! Helping biological families to withdraw their consent to allow the attorney's clients to adopt the biological family's child injures the adoptive family. They have money wrapped up in this adoption, and the attorney just helped another torpedo the case. If, on the other hand, the attorney refuses to assist the biological family in revoking their consent, the attorney's ability to perform the legal service for the biological family already in progress is limited by the attorney's relationship with the adoptive family. This is a conflict of interest with grave implications.

Let's assume for the sake of argument that the biological parents and adoptive parents are comfortable with the conflict of interest and are willing to waive it. Is that permissible? Rule 1.7 allows attorneys to continue in a case when both sides are willing to waive the conflict if "the representation does not involve the assertion of a claim by one client against another client represented by the lawyer in the same litigation or other proceeding before a tribunal." In the case of an adoption, the attorney represents a client claiming the child born to another client who happens to have a Constitutional right to raise that child. This isn't a case of one client suing another for money; it's far graver than that. This is a case of one client suing another for a child. This is a conflict that cannot be waived.

As a result, another solution here is for adoptive and biological parents to file ethics complaints against attorneys who represent both sides of a case, and for governing authorities to discipline those attorneys by a reprimand, suspension, or if the case is so egregious as to warrant it, a disbarment. In my jurisdiction, it took 62 criminal charges against an attorney in three jurisdictions before action was taken to discipline the attorney. The legal profession is self-governing. These cases are doing much harm to the American citizens the bar serves. It is time for lawyers to discipline themselves to stop this type of dual representation.

The question then arises as to whether one firm or agency can handle an entire adoption internally. I do think it is possible if there are sufficient protections in place to guard the independence of each professional representing and advocating for each party to the adoption pyramid. In the law, we call this a Chinese Wall. All access to each other's files is cut off. Each person is held to the highest standards of confidentiality despite working in the same office.

There are situations in which even a Chinese Wall does not work in law firms, but I think it can work in an adoption agency. There can be an attorney or social worker assisting each party in the pyramid with the same protections of professional independence and confidentiality.

That may not be wise, though. There can always be allegations of a conflict of interest regardless of the protections in place, and no security system is perfect. There will be mistakes, and on occasion, it is possible that despite the protections, a conflict occurs. In that case, it is wisest to focus on helping one party. A law firm can focus on assisting the adoptive parents since an attorney must file the appropriate paperwork with the courts. An agency with a background in social work can help biological parents. The attorney and agency can agree on an attorney ad litem or independent social worker to advocate for the best interests of the child by a home study that is more robust than one or two meetings. That process should be ongoing throughout the entire span of the adoption plan from beginning to end. Both adoptive and biological families should have access to the child's advocate to discuss concerns.

This does not constitute a drastic change from the current system. Agencies are already involved in the process. Attorneys are already engaged in the process. The key is merely changing from a situation in which the agency hires the adoptive parents' lawyer or having a list of "preferred" lawyers. Adoptive parents hire their own lawyers and pay less to the agency. Adoptive parents pay a social worker or attorney ad litem directly after agreeing with the biological parents on who that person should be. Whether agencies, social workers, or attorneys, everyone in the pyramid should have their own adoption practitioner, who is solely loyal to them to avoid conflicts of interest.

There have been other proposals that would at least help stave off the adverse consequences of a conflict of interest. One such proposal was to require the professional to disclose the fact that they represent both sides of the case and whether they have represented one party in a previous adoption. This is not the best course of action. The objection was based primarily on the lack of confidentiality of the parties if a practitioner were required to disclose a conflict. I do not believe this involves a breach of confidentiality. The practitioner does not have to disclose names if confidentiality is an issue. The practitioner only has to reveal that he or she had previously represented the other party in an adoption and get everyone to sign off that the practitioner represents and aids both sides.

Despite that fact, this arrangement still fails to account for the best interests of the child. No one is working to ensure the child is the priority in the case; the pyramid stands to suffer foundational damage. Additionally, it does not end the conflict of interest; it only tells those who could suffer because of it that a conflict exists. There will be some who do not know what a conflict of interest means. Statistically, there will still be conflicts that harm adoptive and biological families, and by extension, the child. It is better than the system we have now, but it does not adequately solve the problem.

Eliminating conflicts of interest is a goal which, when achieved, will move the needle towards ethical adoptions the most. When each party to an adoption has a loyal advocate, the pyramid stands the highest chance of maintaining its shape. When each has an advisor, the system is transformed to reflect payment for the service of professionals rather than making adoption agencies look like consignment shops. When each party has a suitable voice, proper adoption and pregnancy-related expenses stand a higher chance of being paid, and improper expenses stand a higher chance of never finding their way to an expense report. Each advocate can then hold the others accountable to the highest standards of ethical conduct. In terms of reform, ending conflicts of interest should be a priority.

IV
Paying for a Child

One of the more controversial issues in adoption law is the payment of money from an adoptive parent to biological parents in connection with the adoption. Internationally the practice of money changing hands between adoptive and biological parents is frowned upon, going so far as to attempt to regulate even domestic adoptions. Enforcing this treaty obligation under our federalist system of government seems complicated; adoption has historically been primarily a matter of state law.

Adding complexity to the controversy is the hodgepodge of state laws in the nation. More than forty states allow for the payment of expenses from adoptive to biological parents. There are vast differences in how states treat those payments. Some rules prohibit the payment of certain types of expenses. Other states cap the amount which may be paid. Some states require the permission of a court to pay costs and a finding that any given expense is reasonable. Some states limit the time frame in which adoptive parents can make payments. There is little consistency between those states as to how long before birth, an expense can be paid, and how long after delivery one can be paid. Complexity grows even more as states define what expenses are payable in what periods. As such, there is no uniformity across state lines as to what is permissible.

From the outside looking in, it is natural and easy to try and oversimplify the system. Regardless of the system of payments from adoptive to biological parents, one party who will receive the child of another pays the natural parent of that child in connection with the adoption. Without any further distinction, that seems like one party is buying a child from another.

But let us consider the alternatives. As a result of the pregnancy, the biological family will incur expenses. It is no secret that expecting mothers must consume more food than those who are not expecting. As such, food costs go up. From the foundation of the pyramid, prenatal care is a must. Medical expenses go up. To obtain prenatal care, expectant mothers must take time off work; for those who work at an hourly rate, wages are lost. Some expectant mothers will have to travel a decent distance throughout the pregnancy to obtain that prenatal care and will spend more on gas.

For those who choose to grow their family, these costs are not usually questioned. For the sake of their unborn child, they make the sacrifices of lost wages and additional medical and food expenses. But for those who decide that adoption is best for them and their child, it is far less reasonable to expect them to bear the burden of those expenses. If financial factors are the only factors considered, an abortion will most likely be less expensive than an adoption. If factors beyond economics lead an expecting mother to adopt rather than abort, the financial stresses could lead to less frequent prenatal care to avoid lost wages and additional medical expenses.

We must also understand that the decision to place a child up for adoption is not only physically tricky; it is mentally and legally tricky. Since it is right to take care of the physical health of the expecting mother, it is right to take care of her mental health. The negative impact of stress and its psychosomatic effects on an unborn baby is well documented. Postpartum depression is no less of an issue in adoption situations than in more traditional means of family planning. But for the adoption, the expecting family would have no legal expenses. But for the pregnancy and adoption, the biological parents would not have experienced these additional costs.

There are some expenses that it is only fair for adoptive parents to pay. Other categories of costs are far less certain. In my experience with adoption over the last few years, through no fault of the adoptive parents, I have seen expense reports that paid for rent, utilities, gaming systems, cell phone service, birthday parties, and even an entire car. Some of these expenses could be justifiable. If the biological mother is homeless, paying rent so that she may have the basic necessity of shelter seems proper. If the water company plans to shut off the water for non-payment, ensuring the mother has water also seems fitting. I can't imagine when a gaming system would ever be appropriate.

Even those expenses which seem justifiable can quickly become unjustifiable. What should we allow when utility bills go unpaid because an expectant mother purchased a gaming system? What should happen if the expecting mother already has a place to live? Should the adoptive parents assist with rent? In short, should adoptive parents pay for the expectant mothers to rob Peter to pay Paul?

Of proposed solutions to this problem, banning expense payments altogether is not a good solution. It stands to force a worse decision: parenting without the ability to care for the child or abortion. The heart behind this policy solution is pure: no one wants to buy a child. Such practices in the international adoption market are why the international community has striven to ban the payment of expenses. Since the Hague Convention, which seeks to ban these payments, intercountry adoptions have dropped precipitously. This is not due to a decrease in trafficking; it has merely shifted from trafficking through adoption to trafficking in the sex and slave trades.

Capping expenses is a little better. Each adoption case is different. Sometimes, the expense payments one mother need are more than another mother. Medically complicated pregnancies cost more than more routine pregnancies. Expecting mothers in rural communities must travel further to access quality prenatal care, meaning they lose more in wages from being off work and spend more on travel costs. Discrepancies in gas prices from one part of the state to the other are alone sufficient to demonstrate the lack of uniformity from case to case, which a cap on expenses assumes.

One solution has been to provide a relief valve of sorts by allowing the parties to request the permission of a judge to exceed the cap. Naturally, that would also increase legal expenses. The increase in costs could lead to disagreements in expenses. This is especially true in light of the fact many practitioners worry that a cap on expenses would amount to an advertisement of how much a biological family can get. Biological parents would come to rely on the fact that they would receive the full amount of the cap, while adoptive parents would come to rely on the cap as the maximum which they would spend. Both create problems.

Another solution that I have advocated in the past is judicial oversight of all such payments. There are a couple of different ways this could happen. One is the practice of filing the adoption petition as soon as a match is made and prohibiting all such support payments until a petition is filed. At that point, the court can immediately begin supervising the process. To avoid a judicial backlog, the law could allow for the court to appoint a trustee in much the same fashion as a trustee is appointed in bankruptcy or receivership. In essence, the trustee would act as an escrow agent with authority to make independent decisions regarding the propriety of an expense. While this provides oversight of the process much better than current systems, it will raise the cost of adoption by increasing time in court or the fees of the trustee. That accountability could be provided by doing away with conflicts of interest to a degree.

Another possibility is to require biological mothers to keep receipts on which the adoptive parents can provide reimbursement for legitimate expenses. There are several problems with this approach, as well. First, most biological parents who find themselves in a place where adoption is necessary find it challenging to keep receipts. Many times, people in this position have a degree of financial illiteracy that would make any degree of bookkeeping and reconciliation impractical. This approach also fails to address the problems of biological families' discretionary spending in excessive amounts to artificially inflate their perceived need.

For those states that allow expenses, the problem is often in the definitions. What does it mean that housing expenses are permissible? Does that mean all housing expenses during the pregnancy or only housing expenses that increase as a result of the pregnancy? Or does it mean only those housing expenses that are in the best interest of the unborn child? If it is unethical for a biological family to profit from the adoption of their child, we cannot define housing expenses to cover all rent under almost every circumstance except the homelessness of the biological mother or abusiveness of the biological father. This is only one example of many, which demonstrates the need to better define the payment of expenses from adoptive to biological parents.

Herein lies the best solution, in my opinion. A lack of clarity about what is permissible and impermissible creates a breeding ground for the efforts of my kindred: lawyers looking for any loophole they can find. In my home state of Arkansas, payments are allowed for a biological mother's "general maintenance." What does that mean? Arkansas case law does not define it well. It is used primarily in terms of alimony and child support. To that extent, it could be as I have argued it should be understood earlier in this chapter: payments necessary to offset expenses incurred as a result of a pregnancy ending in adoption. However, some would argue that these two words constitute much more. Instead of paying the increase in expenses, adoptive parents could pay all a biological family's rent and utilities under their definition of the words. If they do not use "general maintenance" to justify such expenses, they use the fact that housing costs and food are specifically called out that justify those payments. The argument is that "general maintenance" does not further describe reasonable payments; it is a separate category of expense. This lack of clarity has caused a wide disparity in terms of what expenses are paid. In some parts of Arkansas, adoption expenses are only a few thousand dollars (so much so that a proposed $10,000 cap was rejected as excessive). In other parts of the state, more than $15,000 in payments are justified and approved. Such disparities should not exist.

We should not end the payment of expenses altogether. Doing so would lead to a further decline in adoptions and could reverse the downward trends of abortion numbers. However, we must not continue with the wild west, zero accountability system that currently exists in many states. No parent should profit from the adoption of their child. Ideally, a biological family would only receive from the adoptive parents that amount of money above their average monthly expenses. Adoption is a legal decree that a child was born to the adoptive parents; it is as if the relationship between the biological parent and child never existed legally. The child cannot inherit or necessarily receive support from the biological family. Payments from adoptive parents to biological parents should have the same effect. They should not profit from the situation, but they also should not suffer financial harm from the additional expenses related to pregnancy and adoption.

Instead, we must better define what is considered appropriate. We must anticipate those additional expenses and allow payments in that category. The increase in medical and legal fees, food, travel, lost wages, and similar expenses should always be permissible. Most of the time, housing and utilities are not an issue and should not be paid. In some cases, though, these expenses should be allowed for the health of the mother and child. However, there must be a stop-gap to prevent unscrupulous biological parents increasing discretionary expenses to justify profiting from the adoption of their child.

Three issues arise under this framework of better definitions. First, there must be a means of determining when unusual payments are permissible. When there are no conflicts of interest, the agency assisting the biological parents can advocate for those expenses to be paid and should be working to obtain other human services to get the family off the streets without expense to the adoptive family. Relying on adoptive family expenses is too temporary a fix not to pursue more long term, social services assistance.

The second issue is determining when a biological family is manipulating the situation to garner additional payments from the adoptive families. Once again, removing conflicts of interest fix problems in the payment of expenses that are not common to every adoption case. When a separate professional represents the adoptive parents, that professional can screen requests for extraordinary payments for fraudulent situations.

The third issue deals with enforcement. The law already requires parties to report expenses to the state in some fashion, usually through the court. In many circumstances, however, there are no enforcement mechanisms available. The Court could deny the adoption due to improper payments, but that creates a bigger problem in that a) the adoptive parents are out thousands of dollars (and not always within the knowledge of the adoptive parents) and b) the biological family has already indicated an inability to care for the child. This likely would remove a child to state custody, which is not a good outcome.

The better outcome is to have a means of holding those responsible for managing payments from adoptive to biological families accountable for the decisions they make. If the adoptive parents are making all decisions as to whether a payment should be made, the adoptive parents should be held to account for those decisions which are improper. When an attorney or agency decides as to the propriety of a payment, that attorney or agency must be held accountable. The question is how to do that. Should the biological parents repay the money? Should their attorney or agency be responsible for paying it back? Should the adoptive parents or their attorney be held accountable for making improper payments? If so, how would they be held responsible since they cannot pay themselves back?

The answers to these questions must be equitably made. Whoever is culpable must be held accountable. If the biological parents fraudulently increase discretionary spending to claim an inability to keep the heat on in their home, they should have to repay that money to the adoptive parents because of their fraud. If the adoptive parents, for some reason, knowingly make an improper payment, there should be civil penalties or criminal sanctions. If an attorney or agency is responsible for negligently or knowingly engaging in improper transfers, they should have to pay the aggrieved parties. As a last resort, the courts should be available to guide what is appropriate, so long as the law that the judge must interpret is clear.

V
National Standards

In November of 2016, National Council for Adoption Executive Direct Chuck Johnson issued a national call for higher ethical standards in the practice of professional adoptions. Recognizing the corruption that has plagued the adoption industry, he called for the highest standards of integrity. Acknowledging the difficulty in identifying where the agency's loyalties lay, he called for agencies to serve every member of the adoption pyramid and greater collaboration between agencies. Repeatedly reminded that members of the adoption pyramid don't know what they don't know, he called for lifelong service to families touched by adoption. Seeing the veritable kaleidoscope of adoption laws from state to state, he called for greater uniformity in the practice of adoption.

In the late 1960s and 1970s, states across the nation passed the Revised Uniform Adoption Act (RUAA) written by the Uniform Law Commission (ULC). Some states changed it. Others have since repealed it and written their own laws. As of the writing of this book, only five states still followed RUAA. The remaining forty-five states and other U.S. jurisdictions have their own adoption laws. ULC has since drafted another uniform adoption law. No states have passed it.

Before the ratification of the Hague Convention, adoption was becoming increasingly global. Every country has its own unique system and understanding of adoption. The regulatory difficulties associated with the Hague Convention has served to reverse the global trends in adoption. As adoptions go, those which occur outside of the family are becoming increasingly interstate (although due to ethical issues adoption numbers, in general, continue to subside). Combined with the mosaic of adoption laws from state to state, the chances of any given interstate adoption being governed by two different sets of laws are over ninety-eight percent. This is unnecessarily complicated.

Speaking of unnecessarily complicated, the states got together in an attempt to rectify the panoply of adoption laws by passing the Interstate Compact on the Placement of Children (ICPC). ICPC gets state agencies involved and does little to ensure an ethical process. Ultimately, it does little more than add bureaucratic red tape.

The federal government has been hesitant to do much with adoption because adoption, like other family law, is inherently a state issue over which the federal government has no jurisdiction. By a strictly federalist interpretation, that may be true. However, it fails to recognize the marketplace that is private adoption. We have already established that adoptions in almost every state are market-driven. We have found that the vast majority of them are interstate in nature. As such, the Commerce Clause of the U.S. Constitution comes into play.

The Commerce Clause gives the federal government the ability to regulate commerce "among the several states." The application of the commerce clause to justify the federal government's regulation requires very little. For example, in 2005, the Supreme Court upheld the federal government's control of growing medical marijuana for personal consumption under state law under the Commerce Clause because there could be an indirect effect on interstate commerce even if no marijuana or money crossed state lines. Almost invariably, money will cross state lines in an interstate adoption. The federal government has the power to govern adoption by legislation or executive regulation. This is the first means by which national standards for adoption practice could be set.

Federal regulation of adoption is not without its problems. Federal procedures take place in federal courts. If the federal government is to pass its own procedural guidelines, the federal courts would likely have to hear adoption cases. That is extraordinarily unlikely. The remaining method of governing adoptions is through the power of the purse. Federal subsidies to states can be conditioned upon the states adopting specific laws or procedures. The federal government could set out national standards for adoption practice and partially fund the state regulatory agencies who follow those standards. If the states do not implement those standards, the states do not get the money. Typically, the states will be quick to pass those laws and get the money, especially if the cause is just and relatively uncontroversial.

Another means of providing national standards is to attempt another uniform law or amending ICPC. There are several difficulties with this approach. Federal legislation that establishes national standards for adoption practitioners must go through one congress and the President. The current state of affairs in Washington tee that up as a tall order. However, amending ICPC or drafting another uniform law must be passed through fifty congresses and fifty governors. When the 1994 Uniform Adoption Act came out of ULC, some states were hesitant to consider it because they had just drafted their own adoption laws. These states did not necessarily even object to the text of the proposed legislation (although there were plenty of objections to go around within the adoption profession). If those objections within the adoption community are addressed, then it is at least possible for new uniform legislation to work. However, based on the panoply of approaches to adoption state by state, this is far too inefficient and unlikely to accomplish uniformity in national standards.

Another solution is for state regulatory authorities to adopt ethical standards. There are multiple regulatory models followed from state to state, but there are regulatory and administrative rules that licensed child welfare agencies must follow. Those rules could be used to establish ethical standards for all agencies to follow. Generally speaking, it is easier for regulatory authorities to make rules than it is for legislatures to do so. However, this option would still require fifty different regulatory bodies to pass similar ethical standards. Federal legislation could still be easier, as could federal regulations through the Department of Health and Human Services.

The question remains as to what standards should exist. Johnson almost got it entirely right. He called for equal service to all members of the adoption pyramid and greater collaboration between agencies as a means of resolving the ill-effects of a conflict of interest. What he should have called for was a national end to those conflicts of interest.

Uniform post-adoption service requirements for adoptive and biological parents would also be beneficial. There is a tendency to treat biological parents often like a supply chain. One result of this is that frequently they are forgotten as soon as the adopted child is born. In the worst-case scenarios I've been involved in, pregnant women were brought from overseas for the sole purpose of adoption. They often do not speak English. After they give birth, they are kicked to the proverbial curb. Having no command of the language, poor job skills, poor education, and no prospects of the better life they were promised, they do the only thing they know how to get money: get pregnant and enter into an adoption plan. They get stuck in a cycle of pregnancy and adoption.

Only post-adoption services would help them have any prospect of breaking that cycle. There are a host of social services these families should be provided. There are charitable organizations that would provide basic job training. Others could offer services that would lead to a GED if necessary. There are family planning services that many organizations provide. Each of these services does not necessarily cost the adoptive or biological families any money, operating instead on charitable donations. Those who object to such services often fail to remember that adoption should never occur. Adoption happens when a family breaks. Any other understanding of the situation almost invariably reflects an adoption pyramid turned on its head. At least as a perk, though, studies show that birth mothers who were considering abortion had positive adoptions instead, at least in part because the pro-life community embraced them. For an open adoption to work, everyone must have access to post-adoption services. These are as good an argument as any for providing ongoing support.

Some will hear the stories in this book, and the words 'human trafficking' will come to mind. Humans are trafficked through adoption courts on a fairly regular basis – much more than anyone knows or would be comfortable with. One of the best ways to fix that is to have uniform jurisdiction and venue laws. Jurisdiction laws establish guidelines for what state has the jurisdiction to hear a case based on the residency of the adoptive and biological parents. Uniformity in these laws, in conjunction with clarifications in ICPC, could make a big difference in reducing the trafficking of children and biological parents. Venue laws determine which court within the state hears the adoption case. Uniform laws could stave off forum shopping – the practice of choosing courts to get a favorable judge. For those states which still hear adoptions in probate courts, uniform venue laws could move these cases to juvenile courts where they belong.

In the mid 19th Century, adoption was primarily motivated either by a need for labor on the western frontier or the need for a male heir. A deed often finalized adoptions in the same way we transfer real estate. In many states, the vestiges of this system remain in that adoptions are heard in probate courts where property issues are adjudicated after death. Juvenile courts are far more competent to hear these cases with access to social services, child development specialists, and more.

While it should go without saying, national standards of integrity are essential. Stories reflecting a lack of integrity among adoption practitioners are plenty and horrifying. State child welfare agencies have placed sex offenders with adoptive families who had other children. In one case, the adoptive parents specifically asked whether the child had a history of acting out sexually and were told no. That child later sexually assaulted his adoptive parents' other child. It was only then that the adoptive family learned the truth. Adoptive parents have specifically asked about the medical nature of a pregnancy. They were told that it was not a high-risk pregnancy. Just over halfway through the pregnancy, the biological mother went into labor and delivered. Two weeks later, the baby died, and the adoptive parents were left to bury the child they never got to adopt. Only then did they learn that the biological mother (with the knowledge of the adoption professional) was told by medical personnel during her last pregnancy never to get pregnant again because doing so would likely result in a uterine abruption. Two years after one of my own adoptions, I learned that the circumstances of that adoption were greatly exaggerated at best. Integrity is always necessary. While the rampant conflicts of interest exacerbate the results of a lack of integrity, even without the conflicts, both adoptive and biological parents deserve to know the facts and be told the truth by those who get paid to help them.

They also deserve a base degree of competence. Far too many "adoption consultants" with no license or proper training in social work, law, or other adequate training are trying to help people through adoptions. Unfortunately, they do not know what they are doing. Too many adoptions are going to court with things are missing, and the adoption is substantially and unnecessarily delayed. Nationwide there must be harsh penalties for unlicensed adoption practitioners and sanctions for those who are licensed that fail to maintain their competence.

There must be national standards on the reasonableness of fees. Yes, something must be done to deal with the racial price disparities that we've already discussed. At the same time, there are circumstances in which the fee is not reasonable. There are times in which a biological family chooses adoption at the last minute. There are no expenses to care for the family during the pregnancy. There is no overhead and no extensive personnel costs necessary to manage the case during the pregnancy. Yet many agencies will charge the same amount for that adoption as they will for every other adoption. This is simply not reasonable.

There are other ethical areas of professional ethics which should be national in scope, but which are not as much of a problem. There are far fewer complaints involving a lack of confidentiality than other ethical issues. That does not mean there should not be national confidentiality requirements. There aren't many who complain about a lack of diligence by adoption practitioners, but there should still be rules requiring them to be diligent in the performance of their duties.

There are several different branches of ethics. When we talk about ethical procedures and systems in which adoptions take place, we cannot forget to talk about applied professional ethics. Professional adoption ethics must ensure integrity, competency, and loyalty in the adoption process. They must be national in scope. They must be followed and enforced. When they are broken, there must be sanctions.

VI
OPEN ADOPTIONS

I was not initially a proponent of open adoptions. When our first birth mother came to our church to see our adopted child, we were very on edge. There was always a fear in the back of our minds that the mother may take our baby. I learned while researching adoption reform issues that a closed adoption was not in the best interest of my children.

Historically, adoptions were open even when motivated and perfected by unethical means. Starting in the 1930s, states began passing confidentiality and privacy in adoption statutes. It was well-intended. The thought was that such laws would protect kids from the stigma of being illegitimate. But by the time that generation of adoptees reached adulthood, everyone in the adoption pyramid began expressing frustration with nagging, unanswered questions about the adoptee's background.

There are degrees of openness, though. There is no formal or widely accepted definition of what an open adoption is. Instead, they exist on a continuum. Closed or confidential adoptions are at one end of the spectrum. In the middle are mediated adoptions of varying degrees in which the adoption agency or a third-party forwards communication or otherwise acts as an intermediary. Fully disclosed adoptions are on the other end of the spectrum, and even then, some variables make each fully disclosed adoption different. These variations are in the type, frequency, and participants involved in the contact. On top of this, there must be openness between the adoptive parents and adoptee on adoption topics.

Studies have found multiple benefits in open adoptions. Adoptees have first-hand knowledge of the reasons for their adoptions and access to other information that aid in their growth, medical care, and more. Adoptees have access to background information that helps them form their identity. Most adoptees need closure, which studies have shown is at least moderately or very important to about two-thirds of adoptees. Open adoptions help adoptees form positive feelings about their biological mothers and have an additional supportive adult relationship in their lives.

Open adoptions also benefit the biological parents. Birth mothers have significantly faster returns of good mental health. Their feelings of grief and loss after adoption were substantially lower than those in closed adoptions. Also, biological families are more satisfied with their adoption when those adoptions are open. Adoptive parents have positive experiences, as well. None in this particular study reported regret or worry, and 94% reported satisfaction with their open adoption. That satisfaction is even higher when the adoptee participates in contact with the biological parents and has control over the type and frequency of communication, as is age-appropriate. Adoptive parents in open adoptions have a greater feeling of entitlement to parent the adopted child and lower fears of the biological family attempting to take the child back. They have greater empathy and positive attitudes about the biological parents.

Other studies have found similar results. One found that there is a significant, positive association between openness and satisfaction among both adoptive parents and birth parents in addition to birth mothers being able to adjust post-adoption better. In a study of whether adoption messaging had any effect on those seeing an abortion, interesting secondary findings emerged. Out of forty adoptions, the study found twenty-four birth mothers who indicated they had a negative experience in their adoption. Of those, seventeen were closed. The study found twelve birth mothers who reported positive adoption experiences. Only one of them was closed. Also, the study found that birth mothers in closed adoptions were more likely to describe their experience as coercive by their families, the adoptive families, or the agencies they worked with. On the other hand, birth mothers in open adoptions were more likely to describe their experience as one in which they freely chose adoption.

Siegal and Smith also discovered several factors that make open adoptions work well. Open adoptions tend to work better when adoptive and biological parents understand the benefits of open adoption to the adopted child and everyone else as well. Adoptive parents also need to know that open adoption does not erase the loss biological parents face.

Everyone needs to have a shared understanding of what open adoption is and what it is not. There must be a shared understanding of what to expect. Parties must expect that open adoption does not erase the loss biological parents will likely face. They need to understand that open adoption is not a co-parenting arrangement. It is essential to plan for conflicts in open adoptions. It is crucial that everyone has empathy, respect, honesty, and trust in one another, as well as have a commitment to open adoption. Everyone must have a high degree of self-determination. They must have the ability to set boundaries in the relationship as they would in any relationship. Written contracts can help adoptive and biological parents establish trust, demonstrate commitment, and establish boundaries early on. Among adoption agencies, 52% reported that more than 75% of their open adoptions involve a written contract of some type. Only 29% said that less than 25% of their open adoptions involved a written agreement.

However, there is not a "one size fits all" contract that will work. Studies show that at least at the outset, there is an equal amount of loss between birth parents in open adoptions and those in closed adoptions. Others have found that while most adolescent adoptees are happy with or want more contact with their biological families, some kids do not want that contact. There are also situations in which it would not be in a child's best interest to have that contact.

An ethical foundation is also vital to successful open adoption. "Adoptions that are not built on sound, ethical practice are likely to encounter complications down the road, particularly if expecting parents were not supported in exploring their options, were not provided with quality counseling, or were misled or pressured into a decision by their significant others, adoption practitioners, or pre-adoptive parents." Birth parents must be educated about what their rights are, what options they have, and what to expect for their good mental health and the success of open adoption.

There is, therefore, a need for reform in terms of open adoptions. Many states still do not recognize open adoptions. This needs to be the first change. However, reform cannot take place as if permitting open adoptions is the only thing that must be done. The right kind of open adoption must be recognized, and it must be recognized in such a manner as to allow for the unique, individual crafting of agreements in any given situation. At the same time, there are certain aspects of open adoptions that should be required based on the research presented.

For example, pre-adoptive counseling for those choosing an open adoption should be a requirement. Agencies should be required to educate adoptive and biological parents about birth parent grief and loss, the benefits of open adoptions, the need for written agreements, and so forth. Written agreements that set forth the participants, type, and frequency of contact in open adoptions, or that establish that the adoption will be closed or mediated should also be a requirement. Legislation establishing the public policy that open adoptions are favored but are not to be interpreted as co-parenting arrangements is also a necessity. Social and genetic history pleadings that are currently required should be expanded to include as much demographic information as possible regarding the biological parents so that when the time is right, the adoptee has access to that information in the event the adoption ends up closed.

In this book, we have hit on some heavy subjects. Many of us have grown up being taught that adoption is a beautiful thing. It is a noble thing for adoptive parents to take up when done for the right reasons, but that does not diminish the hurt that biological families feel when giving up a child. In the nobility of adoption, there is also corruption. Because too many have seen adoption solely as a means of starting a family, it has become a marketplace. That marketplace was turned gray by unscrupulous adoption practitioners looking to make a buck. They have taken rightfully established support payments meant to make adoption economically neutral and justified exorbitant payments to biological families that are nothing less than the purchasing of a child. In extraordinary cases, it has become nothing less than a black market. Scholars and practitioners have sounded the alarm for almost seventy years, and we've taken few steps to address their concerns.

This is the generation of concerned adoptive parents that can see change. This is the generation of adoptees who can rise up and speak truth to power about what they have been denied through closed adoptions. This is the generation of biological parents who can bring dignity back to adoption. This is the generation in which our society can make adoption what it always should have been – a means of caring for children who need a home.

This cannot be done by legislation alone. There must be a paradigm shift in our society. As such, change is much easier said than done. However, legislation can create a framework for adoption that starts to shift the way we view adoption and approach it. Perhaps as fertility treatments become more effective as research into treatments for infertility advances, we will see demand in the adoption marketplace diminish. Until then, we must continue shaping how adoptions are protected from the unethical conduct of those who are paid to assist those in an adoption plan.

We must go back to placing the child as the foundation of the adoption pyramid, followed by biological families, followed by adoptive parents. We must find ways to change how adoption practitioners are paid and remove the racial, ethnic, age, and similar price disparities from the equation. We must end conflicts of interest in the adoption framework. We must establish national competence and ethical standards for adoption practitioners. We must rethink our post-adoption structure and enforce arrangements that are in the best interests of adoptees. Until we do, nobility will leak out of the broken vessel, which is adoption.

We owe it not only to future adoptees, biological families, and adoptive parents to accomplish these changes. We owe it to ourselves. We owe it to our adopted children. There cannot be another generation of adopted children who grow up one day to understand adoption better only to wonder whether they were purchased. Too many adoptive parents will have tough questions to ask. May our adopted children grow up to see that there was a generation of adoptive parents who stood up to fight for a more ethical, child-focused process!

Made in United States
North Haven, CT
08 January 2022